EASY CRAFTS IN **5** STEPS

Easy Cardboard Crafts in 5 Steps

Enslow Elementary

an imprint of

 Enslow Publishers, Inc.

40 Industrial Road

Box 398

http://www.enslow.com

Note to Kids: The materials used in this book are suggestions. If you do not have an item, use something similar. Use any color material and paint that you wish. Use your imagination!

Safety Note: Be sure to ask for help from an adult, if needed, to complete these crafts.

Note to Teachers and Parents: Crafts are prepared using air-drying clay. Please follow package directions. Children may use color clay or they may paint using poster paint once clay is completely dry. The colors used in this book are suggestions. Children may use any color clay, cardboard, pencils, or paint they wish. Let them use their imaginations!

Enslow Elementary, an imprint of Enslow Publishers, Inc. Enslow Elementary® is a registered trademark of Enslow Publishers, Inc.

English edition copyright © 2008 by Enslow Publishers, Inc.

Translated from the Spanish edition by Ian Grenzeback, edited by Jaime Ramírez-Castilla, of Strictly Spanish, LLC. Edited and produced by Enslow Publishers, Inc.

Library of Congress Cataloging-in-Publication Data

Llimós Plomer, Anna.
  [Cartón. English]
  Easy crafts in 5 steps : easy cardboard crafts in 5 steps / Anna Llimós.
     p. cm.
  Summary: "Presents art projects made with cardboard that can be created in 5 steps"—Provided by publisher.
  Includes bibliographical references and index.
  ISBN-13: 978-0-7660-3083-1
  ISBN-10: 0-7660-3083-0
  1. Box craft—Juvenile literature. 2. Paperboard—Juvenile literature. I. Title. II. Title: Easy crafts in five steps.
  TT870.5.L55 2007
  745.54—dc22
                    2007003413

Originally published in Spanish under the title *Cartón*.
Copyright © 2005 PARRAMÓN EDICIONES, S.A., - World Rights.
Published by Parramón Ediciones, S.A., Barcelona, Spain.
Text and development of the exercises: Anna Llimós
Photographs: Nos & Soto

Printed in Spain

10 9 8 7 6 5 4 3 2 1

To Our Readers: We have done our best to make sure all Internet Addresses in this book were active and appropriate when we went to press. However, the author and the publishers have no control over and assume no liability for the material available on those Internet sites or on other Web sites they may link to. Any comments or suggestions can be sent by e-mail to comments@enslow.com or to the address on the back cover.

Every effort has been made to locate all copyright holders of material used in this book. If any errors or omissions have occurred, corrections will be made in future editions of this book.

Contents

Bee
page 4

Flowers
page 6

Folder
page 8

Mushroom
page 10

Tags
page 12

Watch
page 14

House Box
page 16

Lion
page 18

Drum
page 20

Hand Puppet
page 22

Journal
page 24

Hang-Glider
page 26

Snake
page 28

Cart and Donkey
page 30

Read About & Index
page 32

Bee

Poster board
Corrugated cardboard
Colored pencils
White glue
Scissors
Hole punch
Yarn

1 Draw the body of the bee on poster board. Draw two wings on the smooth part of the corrugated cardboard. Cut out the three pieces.

2 Draw the bee's face with colored pencils.

3 Cut and glue strips of corrugated cardboard on both sides of the bee's body. Cut off any parts that stick out.

4

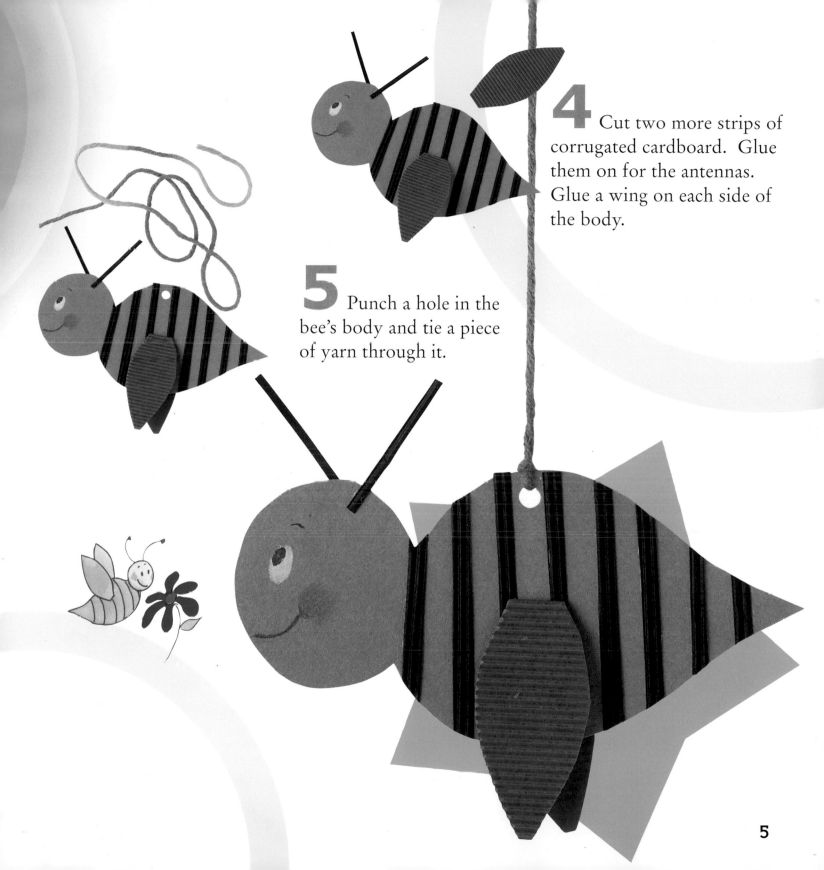

4 Cut two more strips of corrugated cardboard. Glue them on for the antennas. Glue a wing on each side of the body.

5 Punch a hole in the bee's body and tie a piece of yarn through it.

Flowers

MATERIALS

Egg carton
Poster board
Different colors of paint
Paintbrush
Scissors

1 Cut out one of the cups from an egg carton.

2 Paint the cup on the outside and a different color on the inside.

3 Once the paint is dry, paint the cup with stripes.

4 Draw the flower stem on poster board and cut it out. One of the ends should be pointed.

5 Carefully, make a little hole in the bottom of the egg carton cup. Stick the pointed end of the stem into the hole until it is firmly in place.

Folder

MATERIALS

Corrugated cardboard
Poster board
Different colors of paint
Paintbrush, Hook and loop fastener,
White glue, Scissors

1 Cut a rectangle out of corrugated cardboard. Fold it into three parts.

2 Cut out two rectangles of corrugated cardboard. These pieces should be as long as the sides of the folder. Make three folds, like an accordion.

3 Glue these rectangles to the sides of the first rectangle.

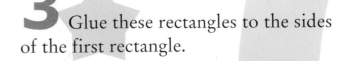

8

4 Draw and cut out two hearts from poster board, one smaller and one bigger. Glue them one on top of the other.

5 Glue the hearts in the middle of the cover. Place the hook and loop fastener on the inside to close the folder.

Mushroom

MATERIALS

Cardboard from a grocery store
fruit container, or paper bowl
Paper towel tube
Corrugated cardboard
Different colors of paint
White glue, Paintbrush
Scissors

1 Cut out one of the cups from the cardboard fruit container. Or use a paper bowl. Paint it on the outside.

2 Once it is dry, decorate it with dots.

3 For the stem, cut off a piece of paper towel tube and paint it.

4 Cut a strip of corrugated cardboard. Cut one side into a wavy shape, and then make little cuts in it to make grass.

5 Glue the strip of grass to one end of the cardboard tube. Glue the cardboard cup to the other.

Tags

MATERIALS

Thick cardboard
Poster board
Corrugated cardboard
Colored pencils
White glue
Hole punch
Ruler
Scissors

1 Draw the shape of a tag on thick cardboard. Draw the same shape, but smaller, on poster board.

2 Cut out the two shapes. Glue the small one on top of the big one. Punch a hole at one end of the tag.

3 Draw a car and wheels on poster board.

12

4 Cut out the pieces and glue them to the tag.

5 Cut out a thin strip of corrugated cardboard. Thread it through the hole.

Watch

MATERIALS

Corrugated cardboard
Cardboard
Colored pencils
Black marker
Hook and loop fastener
White glue
Compass (to draw a circle)
Scissors

1 Cut out a strip of corrugated cardboard to fit around your wrist (the watchband).

2 Use the compass to draw two circles on cardboard. Make one circle smaller than the other.

3 Draw the numbers and the hands of the clock face on the smaller circle. Cut both circles out, and glue the smaller one on top of the bigger one.

4 Glue the clock face to the middle of the watchband.

5 Glue two pieces of hook and loop fastener to the ends of the watchband to fasten the watch.

15

House Box

MATERIALS

Thick cardboard
Egg carton that holds six eggs
Corrugated cardboard
Different colors of paint
Clear tape
Paintbrush
White glue
Scissors

1 Trim off the sides of the egg carton and paint it on the outside.

2 Draw and cut the walls and floor of the house out of thick cardboard. The length of the walls should match to the edges of the egg carton. Glue the walls to the floor with white glue.

3 Paint the ground and the walls of the house. Paint grass and flowers.

4 Cut a door and windows out of corrugated cardboard. Glue them to the house.

5 Use clear tape to attach the painted egg carton (the roof) to one of the long sides of the house.

Lion

MATERIALS

Toilet paper tube
Poster board
Colored pencils
White glue
Scissors

1 Draw the shape of the lion's face on poster board. Draw his mane on another piece of poster board. Make sure the face and mane cover one end of the toilet paper tube.

2 Cut out both pieces. Glue the face on the mane. Cut a nose out of poster board and glue it on.

3 With the colored pencils, draw the lion's face and decorate the ends of his mane.

4 Cut the lion's four legs and tail out of poster board. You can draw hair on the tail and make a few little cuts.

5 Glue all the parts of the lio... to the cardboard tube.

Drum

MATERIALS

Ring of stiff cardboard
Construction paper
Different colors of paint
Clothespins
Colored pencils
Paintbrush
White glue
Scissors

1 Paint the outside of the cardboard ring.

2 Trace the ring on the construction paper. Draw triangles sticking out all around the circle. Cut out the shape.

3 Glue this shape over the cardboard ring, bending the triangles down. You can hold it together with clothespins while the glue is drying.

4 Finish decorating the drum with different color circles.

5 Roll up and glue two long strips of corrugated cardboard for the drumsticks.

21

Hand Puppet

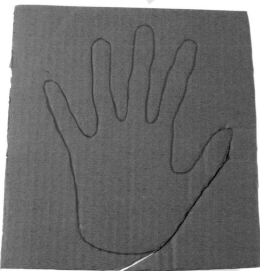

1 Draw the outline of your hand on thick cardboard and cut it out.

MATERIALS

Thick cardboard
Corrugated cardboard
Different colors of paint
Paintbrush and sponge
Scissors
White glue
Colored pencils

2 Paint the fingers.

3 Paint the eyes, nose, and mouth with a paintbrush and the cheeks with a sponge.

4 Cut a strip of corrugated cardboard. Glue the ends together to form a ring that fits on your hand.

Glue the ring to
the back of the
cardboard hand.

23

Journal

MATERIALS

Thick cardboard
Poster board
Corrugated cardboard
White glue
Scissors
Ruler
Black marker
Different colors of paint
Paintbrush

1 Draw two rectangles on the thick cardboard and two more on the poster board.

2 Cut out the four pieces. Glue the poster board to the thick cardboard.

3 Cut a wide strip of corrugated cardboard. Use it to attach the rectangles, like the binding of a book.

4 Draw and cut a circle and eight petals out of corrugated cardboard.

5 Glue the pieces of the flower in the center of one of the covers of the notebook to decorate it. Place some paper inside.

Hang-Glider

1 Cut the tube in half, with one half a little bigger than the other. Make a hole in the center of the bigger piece (the hang-glider).

2 Paint the hang-glider. Let dry. Cut a piece of elastic string and thread it through the hole. Tie a knot.

3 Cut two narrow strips of corrugated cardboard. Fold them in half and glue them to the ends of the hang-glider.

4 Draw the outline of a person on the small half of the cardboard tube. Paint it.

5 Cut the person out and place it on the hang-glider straps.

Snake

MATERIALS

Cardboard from grocery store fruit container,
or egg carton
Poster board
Different colors of paint
Clear tape
Scissors
Paintbrush
Colored pencils

1 Cut a row out of the fruit container.

2 Decorate the body of the snake with paint. Paint two eyes on the head.

3 Paint the pupils. Finish decorating the snake with dots and circles of different colors.

28

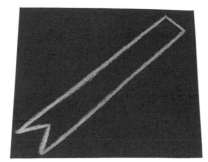

4 Draw and cut the snake's tongue out of poster board.

5 Attach the tongue with clear tape to the back of the cardboard strip, letting it stick out.

Cart and Donkey

MATERIALS

Thick cardboard
Corrugated cardboard
Poster board
Colored pencils
White glue
Scissors

1 Cut two semicircles (the wheels) out of poster board, fold them near the straight edge, and glue them to opposite edges of a square piece of thick cardboard.

2 Cut out a wide strip of corrugated cardboard. Glue it to the other side of the cardboard square like it was the canvas cover for the cart.

3 Cut two long narrow strips and one shorter strip out of corrugated cardboard. Glue the long ones to the canvas and join them together with the shorter one.

4 Draw the donkey's body and legs on a piece of poster board. Make some small slots to put the pieces together.

5 Paint the details of the donkey, cut out the pieces, and put them together.

Read About

Books

Souter, Gillian. *Odds 'n' Ends Art*. Milwaukee, Wis.: Gareth Stevens Pub., 2002.

Wallace, Mary. *I Can Make That!: Fantastic Crafts for Kids*. Toronto, Canada: Maple Tree Press, 2005.

Walsh, Danny, Jake, and Niall. *The Cardboard Box Book: 25 Things to Make and Do with an Empty Box*. New York: Watson-Guptill, 2006.

Internet Addresses

Crafts for Kids at Enchanted Learning
<http://www.enchantedlearning.com/crafts/>

Kids Craft Weekly
<http://www.kidscraftweekly.com/>

Index
E a s y   t o   H a r d

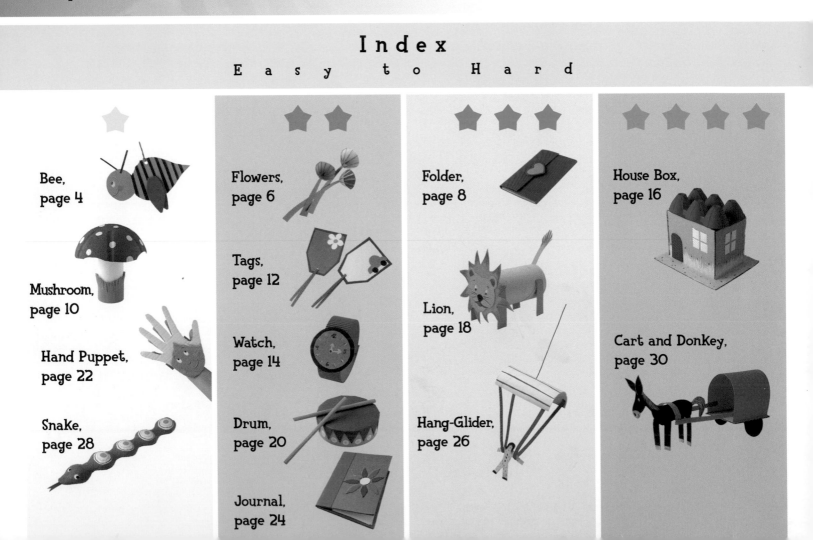

Bee, page 4

Mushroom, page 10

Hand Puppet, page 22

Snake, page 28

Flowers, page 6

Tags, page 12

Watch, page 14

Drum, page 20

Journal, page 24

Folder, page 8

Lion, page 18

Hang-Glider, page 26

House Box, page 16

Cart and Donkey, page 30